PROTEINS

PROTEINS

BY DR. ALVIN SILVERSTEIN, VIRGINIA SILVERSTEIN, AND ROBERT SILVERSTEIN

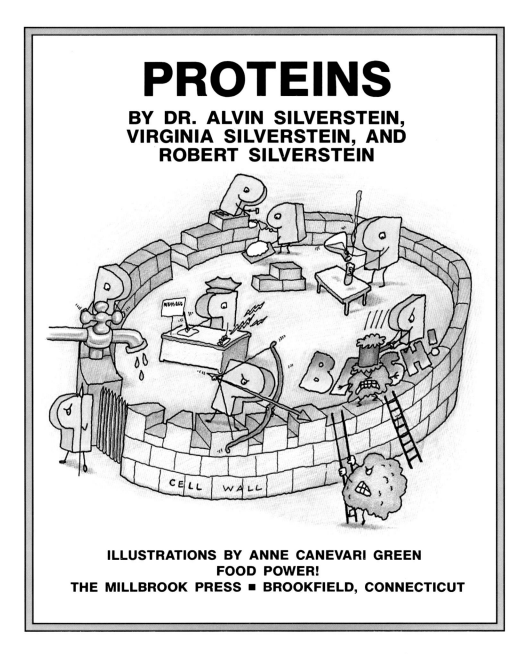

ILLUSTRATIONS BY ANNE CANEVARI GREEN
FOOD POWER!
THE MILLBROOK PRESS ■ BROOKFIELD, CONNECTICUT

Library of Congress Cataloging-in-Publication Data

Silverstein, Alvin.
Proteins / by Alvin, Virginia, and Robert Silverstein;
illustrations by Anne Canevari Green.

p.   cm.—(Food power!)
Includes bibliographical references and index.
Summary: Explains the function of proteins in our body,
how we can get protein, and what amino acids are.
ISBN 1-56294-209-3 (lib. bdg.)
1. Proteins in human nutrition—Juvenile literature.
[1. Proteins.]   I. Silverstein, Virginia B.   II. Silverstein,
Robert.   III. Green, Anne Canevari, ill.   IV. Title.
V. Series: Silverstein, Alvin.   Food power!
QP551.S565   1992
612.3′98—dc20   91-41230   CIP   AC

CONTENTS

YOUR BODY IS JUST LIKE A FACTORY

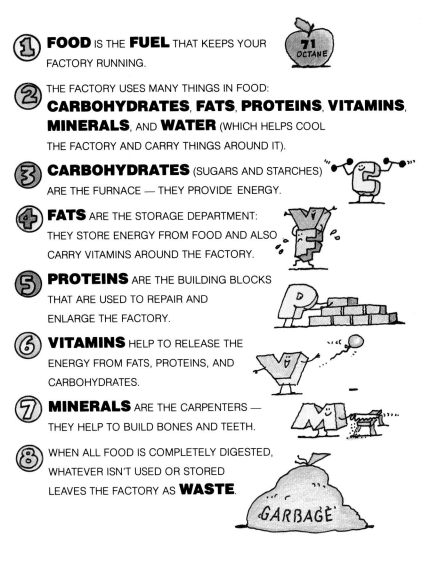

1. **FOOD** IS THE **FUEL** THAT KEEPS YOUR FACTORY RUNNING.

2. THE FACTORY USES MANY THINGS IN FOOD:
CARBOHYDRATES, **FATS**, **PROTEINS**, **VITAMINS**, **MINERALS**, AND **WATER** (WHICH HELPS COOL THE FACTORY AND CARRY THINGS AROUND IT).

3. **CARBOHYDRATES** (SUGARS AND STARCHES) ARE THE FURNACE — THEY PROVIDE ENERGY.

4. **FATS** ARE THE STORAGE DEPARTMENT: THEY STORE ENERGY FROM FOOD AND ALSO CARRY VITAMINS AROUND THE FACTORY.

5. **PROTEINS** ARE THE BUILDING BLOCKS THAT ARE USED TO REPAIR AND ENLARGE THE FACTORY.

6. **VITAMINS** HELP TO RELEASE THE ENERGY FROM FATS, PROTEINS, AND CARBOHYDRATES.

7. **MINERALS** ARE THE CARPENTERS — THEY HELP TO BUILD BONES AND TEETH.

8. WHEN ALL FOOD IS COMPLETELY DIGESTED, WHATEVER ISN'T USED OR STORED LEAVES THE FACTORY AS **WASTE**.

WHAT ARE PROTEINS?

Most people know that you need protein for big, strong muscles. Actually, though, proteins are found throughout the body, from your head to your toes.

There are about 100,000 different kinds of proteins in your body. You need protein to grow, to heal, and to carry out just about every chemical reaction that goes on inside you. Many proteins are building materials for body structures, such as the hair and skin. The proteins in your muscles are strong and stretchy, like rubber bands. Proteins give shape and strength to organs such as the heart, lungs, and brain.

Why are they called proteins?

Protein comes from the Greek word *proteios*, meaning "primary" or "holding the first place." These important chemicals were first named back in 1838. Since then we have learned a lot about what proteins do in our bodies. They are certainly well named!

Some body proteins travel around. Hemoglobin, a protein in blood, carries oxygen to all parts of the body. Many hormones, which act as the body's chemical messengers, are proteins. Enzymes are proteins that help other chemicals in the body to react. Without them you couldn't breathe, digest your food, or even think. Proteins called antibodies fight germs and help to keep you healthy.

All the many kinds of proteins in your body have one thing in common. They are all chemicals made up of 20 kinds of simple building blocks, called *amino acids.*

AMINO ACIDS: THE BUILDING BLOCKS

The proteins in your body come in many sizes and shapes. The simplest ones look a little like trains, with many cars linked together. Each "car," or unit, in a protein is an amino acid.

The Amino Acid "Alphabet"

Millions of proteins are found in nature, but most proteins contain only 20 different amino acids. How can this be? Well, there are millions of words in the English language, but they can all be spelled out with an alphabet of just 26 letters. The many different "messages" in proteins are spelled out in a similar way, using an "alphabet" of amino acids in millions of different combinations.

All living creatures—animals, plants, even bacteria—have their own proteins, spelled out in the amino acid alphabet. Some of the proteins in your body are almost exactly the same as those in a dog or a frog or a sunflower. But some kinds of proteins are found only in humans. In

These are the 20 amino acids in human proteins

Alanine	(A)	*Leucine	(L)
Arginine	(R)	*Lysine	(K)
Asparagine	(N)	*Methionine	(M)
Aspartic acid	(D)	*Phenylalanine	(F)
Cysteine	(C)	Proline	(P)
Glutamic acid	(E)	Serine	(S)
Glutamine	(O)	*Threonine	(T)
Glycine	(G)	*Tryptophan	(W)
*Histidine	(H)	Tyrosine	(Y)
*Isoleucine	(I)	*Valine	(V)

*Essential amino acids, which our bodies can't make from other chemicals.

Using the amino acid alphabet

Glue a sheet of blank paper to a piece of cardboard, and, using a ruler, draw lines 1 inch apart across and down the sheet. Now you will have 88 boxes.

Print one letter from the list of amino acid abbreviations in each box. You will have enough spaces to go through the whole list four times. Fill up the rest of the boxes with extra vowels, A, E, I, and O. Cut along the lines to separate the letter boxes.

How many different words can you make with your set of amino acid letters? Can you put some of the words together to form sentences?

In real proteins, of course, the amino acids don't spell out any words you'd recognize. But their messages are full of meaning for the body.

fact, some of the proteins in your body may have a slightly different amino acid "spelling" from the same kinds of proteins in other people—for example, your friends or even your parents! These differences in proteins are one reason why the various kinds of animals and plants (and individual people) look so different from each other.

What Are Amino Acids Made Of?

Each amino acid contains the chemical elements carbon, hydrogen, oxygen, and nitrogen. Two of the amino acids, cysteine and methionine, also contain sulfur. Carbohydrates and fats, the other main kinds of food chemicals, contain carbon, hydrogen, and oxygen. But most of them do not have any nitrogen.

The nitrogen atom in an amino acid is linked with two hydrogen atoms to form an *amino group*. All of the amino acids also contain an *acid group*, formed from carbon, hydrogen, and oxygen atoms.

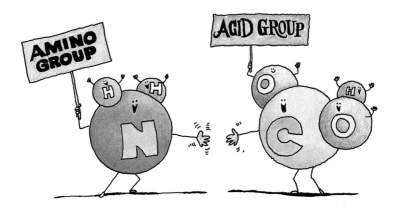

An amino group from one amino acid can join together with an acid group from another amino acid, like a pair of snap-together beads. They form a new compound called a *peptide*, and the chemical connection between them is called a *peptide bond*. But each amino acid in the newly formed peptide still has an acid group or amino group that isn't connected to anything. This free end can react with another amino or acid group to make the peptide chain longer. Some proteins are made up of long chains of amino acids, each linked to the next one by a peptide bond.

The Many Sizes and Shapes of Proteins

Not all proteins look like trains or chains of snap-together beads. Some are rolled up in the shape of a ball. We call these globular proteins. Others form flat plates. Some are coil shaped, some basket shaped. Still others look very much like the letter Y. (These are the antibodies that help us to fight disease-causing germs.)

Some proteins contain more than one chain of amino acids. For example, hemoglobin, the protein that gives blood its red color, is formed by four separate chains linked together.

Some proteins are rather small. The hormone insulin, for instance, contains only 51 amino acids. (Insulin helps to regulate the use of sugar in the body. It was the first protein whose complete amino acid "spelling" was figured out.) But some of the antibody proteins are huge, containing thousands of amino acids.

Testing for proteins

Place a piece of cheese in a test tube. Add 20 drops of a 5 percent solution of copper sulfate. To this, add 20 drops of lime solution. (You can prepare the lime solution by adding a tablespoon of powdered lime [the mineral, not the fruit] to a cup of water.)

If the solution turns violet, then protein is present. (Copper salts react with the peptide bonds in proteins to form violet-colored compounds. Different kinds of proteins may produce different shades.)

Try this experiment with small samples of other foods, too, such as various meats, fish, egg white, milk, potato, apple, and bread. Which ones give a violet color? WARNING: *Do not eat any of the tested foods.*

In some proteins, amino acids are combined with other things. Glycoproteins, for example, contain amino acids and sugars. Lipoproteins have fats. And in nucleoproteins, the peptide chains are joined to chemicals called nucleic acids (DNA and RNA), which carry the body's hereditary instructions.

The Essential Amino Acids

The human liver is able to manufacture 11 of the 20 amino acids from other chemicals. That leaves nine amino acids that we need but cannot make ourselves. We must get them from foods. Scientists call the nine amino acids that our bodies cannot make *essential amino acids.*

FOOD PROTEINS

Meat, eggs, and milk—these are the foods most people would name as good protein sources. Some animal products do contain more protein than many other kinds of foods. But most foods have some protein. In fact, some vegetable products—such as peanuts—actually have more protein, ounce for ounce, than many meats.

Our Protein Needs

Could you get along without food proteins? Not unless you were a plant! Plants can make all the chemicals they need from nature's raw materials—air, water, and salts from the soil.

Some of these salts contain the element nitrogen. (Remember nitrogen? It's the element always found in proteins but not usually found in carbohydrates or fats.) Plants can use the nitrogen in salts to make proteins, but people can't. We have to get nitrogen from the proteins we eat.

Our bodies cannot use food proteins in their natural forms. But when the foods are digested, the proteins are broken down into their amino acids, which can then be used to build human proteins.

The amount of protein we eat is important. We need enough to make building materials, enzymes, and hormones. But not just any old protein will do. Although most foods have some protein, not all food proteins contain all of the essential amino acids we need. Our bodies don't store protein or amino acids. So if one or more amino acids are missing from the food we eat in a particular meal, a lot of the amino acids are wasted.

We can think of the way the body builds protein chains as being a little like stringing beads to make a necklace. Let's say we need a red, a blue, and a yellow bead to make each part of the design. In a jar we have eight red beads and eight blue beads, but only two yellows. After only two sets, we'll run out of yellow beads. We won't be able to make a whole necklace, even though we have 12 beads left over.

When the body tries to make proteins with the wrong mix of amino acids, it can't make all the new proteins we need. The extra amino acids that are left over may be used for energy or changed into fat and stored for future energy needs. Either way, some nitrogen is lost in waste products, mostly in urine.

Complete and Incomplete Proteins

Food proteins that contain all the essential amino acids are called *complete proteins*. Most animal foods, such as meat, poultry, fish, eggs, cheese, and milk, are complete proteins. A few kinds of plant proteins are complete, too. Soybean products such as tofu have proteins that are very much like animal proteins and contain all the essential amino acids. Foods that provide complete proteins are said to be *good-quality protein* sources.

What is the best-quality protein source of all? Eggs. The amino acids in egg protein are almost perfect for human needs. The body can use nearly all of the protein in eggs, without wasting it.

Legumes (beans and peas), nuts, seeds, grains, and vegetables are all good sources of food protein. But their proteins contain only small amounts of one or more essential amino acids. They are called *incomplete proteins*, or *less complete proteins*. Just one of these plant foods cannot supply all our protein needs by itself. In addition, the body cannot digest some plant proteins as completely as it can digest animal proteins. So more of the lower-quality proteins must be eaten to supply the body's needs.

Combining Lower-Quality Proteins to Make Complete Proteins

Since proteins from animal sources are high-quality proteins, does that mean they are better to eat than lower-quality plant proteins?

Not necessarily.

We would have a problem if we ate these foods by themselves. But usually we eat several different types of food together. The proteins from the different foods often *complement* each other. This means that although one food may be low in certain amino acids, another food may have a lot of those particular amino acids. When we eat the two foods together, we get just the right balance.

For example, peanut butter is low in the amino acid methionine. Bread has plenty of methionine, but not very much lysine and isoleucine. Together, as a peanut butter sandwich, they make a complete protein.

In our bead example, we had two yellow beads, eight red and eight blue beads. Let's say we had another jar of beads with eight yellows, two reds and two blue beads. If we tried to make a necklace using the beads from only one jar, we would end up with a very short chain, just two sets long. But if we use both jars of beads, we can make ten complete sets!

Nearly one third of the world's population lives on a mostly vegetarian diet, and they are able to meet their protein needs. Many foods that are eaten together contain the right protein complements.

In Mexico, for example, it is common to eat rice with beans, beans in a corn-based tortilla shell, or beans in wheat flour burrito shells. All these form complementary proteins. In the Middle East, hummus is a paste or dip made from chick-peas and sesame seeds, which complement each other. Oriental dishes of stir-fried vegetables and rice with soy sauce also provide a complete protein source. In India, lentils are the complement for rice. Generally, legumes are complementary to grains, and to nuts and seeds. (Did you know that peanuts aren't really nuts? They're legumes.)

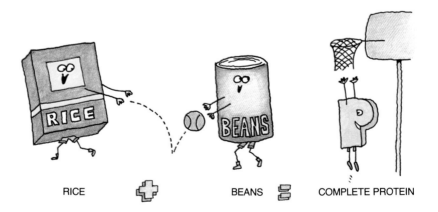

RICE   BEANS   COMPLETE PROTEIN

Combining Incomplete Proteins
With Complete Proteins

Strict vegetarians, who eat no animal products, have to choose their foods very carefully to meet all their protein needs. But some vegetarians eat eggs and milk, in addition to plant foods. It is much easier for them to get enough good-quality proteins in their diet. Mixing an incomplete protein with a complete protein is the easiest way to make sure the incomplete protein can also be used by the body.

Milk is the perfect thing to put in a bowl of cereal, for example. Adding cheese to macaroni allows us to utilize all the macaroni protein.

In many parts of the world, supplies of animal products are very limited. Families can get more nutrition from their food by adding small amounts of meat, poultry, or fish to a grain or vegetable dish. Nutritious combination dishes include tuna casserole, spaghetti and meatballs, beef stew, and chicken chow mein.

Which Protein Foods Are the Best?

A hundred years ago, Americans obtained large amounts of the proteins they needed from flour and cereal products. All together, plant products made up nearly half of the protein supply. If you're like most Americans today, though, you probably have meat at least twice a day, and lots of milk, eggs, and cheese are also in your diet. Most Americans actually eat more than twice as much protein each day as their bodies need.

Meat and dairy products make up nearly three fourths of the protein in our diet. Some health experts say it would be better to get only one third of our protein from animal sources and two thirds from plant sources. Why? Because of the other nutrients that come along with the proteins in the foods we eat.

Other Nutrients in Protein Foods

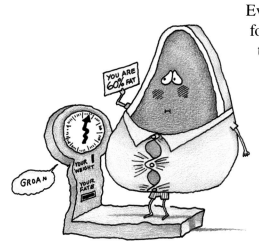

Even the foods that we think of as protein foods may have more of other nutrients than protein. Many animal food products, for example, actually contain more fat than protein. A steak may be from 20 to 50 percent protein (depending on how lean it is) and 50 to 80 percent fat. Hard cheeses, such as cheddar, are about 25 percent protein and 75 percent fat.

In vegetable sources of protein, carbohydrates are often the main nutrient. Kidney beans, for example, are 25 percent protein and 70 percent carbohydrates. (There are a few plant products, such as peanuts, that are very high in fats.)

In addition, plant protein sources usually contain more vitamins, minerals, and fiber than animal products. All these are important parts of the diet and are needed for good health.

Getting the Most Protein
for Your Money

Many people choose plant products over animal ones because they cost less. The protein in beans costs about half as much per pound as the protein in eggs and a quarter the cost of protein in steak.

Some people use meat extenders as a way to make meat go further. You don't need as much meat to make a tasty meat loaf if you add other foods, such as bread, crackers, milk, rice, or oatmeal.

What Happens to Proteins When
Foods Are Cooked?

Have you ever watched an egg frying? The clear slippery liquid spreads out around the yolk when the egg is first poured into the pan. But then, as it is heated, the clear liquid turns into a white solid. The same thing happens when an egg is boiled inside its shell. The egg white becomes quite solid and rubbery. What happened to it?

Egg white is almost pure protein. Heating breaks some of its chemical bonds, and new bonds are formed. The amino acids become linked together into complicated networks instead of long chains. As the egg cooks, these networks tighten, squeezing out some of the water that was trapped inside. The longer you cook the egg, the more water is squeezed out, until the egg white becomes quite hard. Once it is cooked, an egg white will not become liquid again, even if you mix it with water.

Whipping an egg white also breaks chemical bonds, and new bonds are formed. The egg white becomes foamy because air is trapped inside the new protein network. If you cook the whipped egg white, the air expands. The stretchy protein networks in the walls of the bubbles bulge outward and then become firm, forming a soufflé.

Similar changes take place in other food proteins—in a steak while it is broiling, for example. Water is squeezed out when new bonds are formed, and the meat gets smaller when it's cooked.

Why does red meat turn brown when you cook it? Heat breaks down the proteins on the surface and changes them chemically. The brown compounds formed may be tasty, but they do not have as much protein food value. Inside the meat, the color changes from red to brown for a different reason. The red comes from hemoglobin (the protein that gives blood its red color) and a similar protein called myoglobin. Heat breaks down these chemicals and produces the color change.

Why does spoiled meat look green and slimy? Bacteria growing on the meat's surface break down the proteins, forming slime and releasing sulfur compounds. These sulfur compounds give spoiled meat its bad smell. They also react with myoglobin to produce a greenish compound.

WHAT HAPPENS TO THE FOOD YOU EAT?

The organs of the digestive system are like work stations in a factory. Step by step, they prepare food for digestion, break down the nutrients into forms the body can use, and get rid of waste products.

There's acid in your stomach!

The acid in your stomach is called *hydrochloric acid.* Its main function is to help digest proteins, and it is very strong. If you put an iron nail in a cup of gastric juice, the nail would dissolve!

If stomach acid is strong enough to dissolve a nail, why doesn't it dissolve your stomach, too? A protein in gastric juice called *mucin* forms a slippery coating that protects the soft lining of the stomach. If the stomach does not make enough mucin, the acid can form a sore, called an *ulcer*, in the stomach lining.

Did you know . . .

Cats, dogs, and other meat-eating animals don't chew their food! They use their teeth to cut and tear off chunks, then swallow the lumps of meat. The stomach acid and enzymes soften and digest this high-protein food.

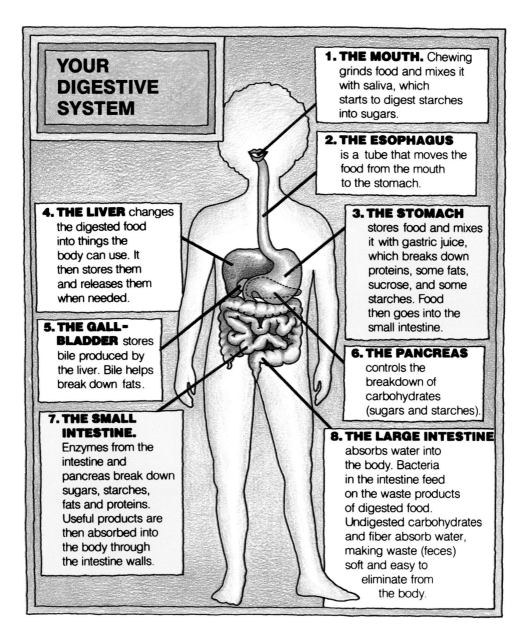

YOUR DIGESTIVE SYSTEM

1. THE MOUTH. Chewing grinds food and mixes it with saliva, which starts to digest starches into sugars.

2. THE ESOPHAGUS is a tube that moves the food from the mouth to the stomach.

3. THE STOMACH stores food and mixes it with gastric juice, which breaks down proteins, some fats, sucrose, and some starches. Food then goes into the small intestine.

4. THE LIVER changes the digested food into things the body can use. It then stores them and releases them when needed.

5. THE GALL-BLADDER stores bile produced by the liver. Bile helps break down fats.

6. THE PANCREAS controls the breakdown of carbohydrates (sugars and starches).

7. THE SMALL INTESTINE. Enzymes from the intestine and pancreas break down sugars, starches, fats and proteins. Useful products are then absorbed into the body through the intestine walls.

8. THE LARGE INTESTINE absorbs water into the body. Bacteria in the intestine feed on the waste products of digested food. Undigested carbohydrates and fiber absorb water, making waste (feces) soft and easy to eliminate from the body.

THE BODY PROTEINS

We've seen how the proteins in the foods we eat are digested and broken down into amino acids. What happens then?

Some amino acids are used for energy or changed into sugars, fats, or other chemicals. But mostly, amino acids are used as building blocks for new proteins. Instead of potato, chicken, or other food proteins, they become *human proteins.*

Except for water, protein is the most common substance in the body. In fact, if you don't count water, proteins make up half of your body tissue! All together, about 18 to 20 percent of the body is protein. Each of the trillions of tiny living cells in your body contains protein. The many kinds of proteins in the body all have their own jobs to do.

A protein called *rhodopsin* in our eyes, for example, helps us to see light. Rhodopsin contains a colored chemical very similar to carotene, which gives carrots their orange color. The *hemoglobin* in red blood cells also contains a colored substance: heme, which gives blood its red color. Hemoglobin carries oxygen from the lungs to the body's cells and takes away their harmful waste product, carbon dioxide.

A series of chemical reactions involving proteins in the blood causes the blood to clot. The clot itself is made up of blood cells, trapped in a network of protein fibers called *fibrin*. Clots help to stop the bleeding when you have a cut. But a blood clot inside a blood vessel could result in a heart attack or a stroke. Other blood proteins help to keep such clots from forming or to dissolve them if they do form.

Do you know what your blood type is? Whether you are A, B, AB, or O is determined by whether your blood contains certain proteins. Police detectives can use tests for these and other body proteins to match up samples of blood or tissues to crime suspects.

The protein factory

Each tiny cell in your body contains a complete set of instructions for making about 100,000 different kinds of proteins. All this information is stored in a chemical called *DNA* (deoxyribonucleic acid), in the form of a code. DNA, like proteins, is made up of long chains. The links on the chains are *nucleotides*. But there are only four main kinds of nucleotides: A, C, G, and T. (Remember, there are 20 kinds of amino acids in human proteins.)

How can only four kinds of nucleotides be the "spelling" instructions for proteins, which have an "alphabet" of 20 amino acids? The same way the two-letter Morse code ("dot" and "dash") can spell out any word in our 26-letter English alphabet: by using combinations. Each group of three nucleotides stands for one kind of amino acid.

Protein Gives the Body Structure

Proteins are the major building blocks for your skin, muscles, cartilage, and internal organs such as the heart, lungs, and brain.

A protein called *keratin*, for example, is made up of strong, waterproof fibers and is found in skin, hair, and nails. Another protein, *collagen*, acts like a glue, holding cells together and strengthening many organs and body tissues. A protein called *elastin* is stretchy, like a rubber band. Elastin in the walls of the blood vessels allows the vessels to expand and contract.

Myosin and *actin* are two other proteins that form stretchy, threadlike fibers. These proteins allow muscles to contract and relax. When you "make a muscle," the bulge in your upper arm is formed by contractions of many tiny protein fibers, all working together.

How to tie a bone into a knot

The next time you eat chicken, save the long leg bones. They seem very hard and stiff. If you tried to bend one, it might break, but it wouldn't bend. Now put the bones in a jar of vinegar. After a few days, take them out. Do they look any different? What happens when you try to bend them?

Bones get their hardness from calcium salts, held in place by a framework made of the protein collagen. Vinegar is an acid. It can dissolve calcium salts, but not collagen. So the bone still keeps its shape, but it is no longer stiff.

Proteins Are Used for
Growth and Repair

Your body is growing every day. New cells are being formed, and various organs and other body parts are developing. Your body is constantly making new proteins to build these structures. It needs continuing supplies of raw materials—the amino acids that you get in protein-rich foods.

Growing children and adolescents need a lot of protein. In fact, they need quite a bit more protein, compared to their weight, than adults do, because adult bodies are not growing anymore.

But adults need protein, too. People who are sick or hurt have to repair or replace body tissues. Even daily living can wear out body cells. Your skin cells are constantly being replaced, for example. You lose some old skin cells every time you wash your hands or scratch your head.

Proteins Help Regulate
Body Processes

This very minute, millions of things are going on inside your body, allowing you to breathe, to see, to hear, and to move. Enzymes, hormones, and other proteins help to control all these processes.

Enzymes help speed up chemical reactions in the body. There are more than 1,000 different types of enzymes in your body. They help in digesting your food, building new proteins, moving muscles and sending messages along

= ENZYMES

= HORMONES

nerves. Without enzymes you couldn't read a book, catch a ball, or sing a song.

Hormones are the body's chemical messengers. They control your growth and development and help to regulate many body activities like breathing and the heartbeat. Many hormones are proteins—for example, human growth hormone. (Guess what job it does!)

Proteins Help Defend the Body

Proteins help to defend you against disease-causing microbes. First of all, they are a key part of your skin, which forms a protective barrier all over your body. Proteins are also a major part of the white blood cells, tiny germ fighters that move through your blood and tissues. And protein *antibodies* attack invading microbes, making them easier for the white blood cells to kill. Antibodies are shaped to fit parts of proteins or other chemicals on the microbes' surface.

Proteins Help Maintain
Our Internal Environment

A blood protein called *albumin* helps to control the amount of water that passes into and out of cells. If you don't eat much protein for several weeks, water will pass out of the blood into the tissues. This may make you look "fat," even though you are actually not getting enough of the food you need.

Other proteins help to keep the acids and bases in the body fluids in just the right balance. Still others act as gatekeepers in the membranes that cover the body's cells, controlling the flow of minerals into and out of the cells.

Protein as an Energy Source

The body can use protein for energy. Proteins give about as much energy as carbohydrates—approximately four calories per gram. But the body will first use carbohydrates or fats if those are available. Using proteins as an energy source is wasteful, because they have so many other important uses as raw materials.

If a person is not eating enough fats and carbohydrates, the body will use protein for energy. In fact, it may not only "burn up" the proteins in foods but may even begin to use body proteins as an energy supply. This is why a very low-calorie reducing diet can be dangerous. Instead of losing fat, the dieter may lose proteins from the muscles and even the heart!

If you eat too much protein, your body can use it for energy. But if you are getting enough carbohydrates and fats, the extra protein will be changed into fat instead and stored away. The body can't store protein for future needs. Yet, as we have seen, proteins are needed for practically everything that goes on in the body. So it is important to eat the right amount and the right kinds of proteins each day.

PROTEINS FOR GOOD HEALTH

As we have seen, proteins are an extremely important nutrient—for growth, for maintaining body structure, and for many of the reactions that go on inside of us. But how much protein does a person need to eat each day to keep everything running just right?

There's no simple answer to that question. In fact, health experts used to think people needed more protein than they now recommend. The 1989 dietary guidelines suggest that 15 percent of your daily calories should come from protein, 30 percent from fat, and 55 percent from carbohydrates.

Not All Protein Needs Are the Same

The exact amounts that are needed vary for different people. For example, the recommended daily allowance (RDA) for a 62-pound child is about 28 grams (112 calories) of high-quality protein per day. Teenagers need from 44 to 59 grams of protein each day, and adult protein needs range from about 46 to 63 grams. Why are there such differences?

In general, larger people need more protein than smaller ones. Children are much smaller than adults, but they have special protein needs, because their bodies are still growing. So infants and children actually need two to three times more protein per body weight than adults do. Pregnant women also need extra protein, for the developing baby.

Men need more protein than women. Why? First of all, the average man is bigger than the average woman. (Remember, larger people need more protein.) In addition, men usually have more muscle, and protein is needed to maintain muscle tissue.

Older people have special needs, too. They often have trouble digesting protein, so they may need to eat more to get the same protein nourishment.

Protein needs also vary depending on how hot it is (sweating carries nitrogen out of the body, and it has to be replaced) and how much exercise you are getting (protein is needed to build muscles). If you're injured or sick, you need extra protein to repair tissues and fight germs. Vegetarians may need to eat extra protein to make sure that they are getting all of the essential amino acids.

Health Problems From Consuming Too Much Protein

Most Americans eat *too much* protein. The average child in the United States eats twice the recommended daily allowance. The average middle-aged American man eats 60 percent more than the *recommended dietary allowance (RDA)* for his weight, and the average middle-aged woman eats 25 percent more.

Usually, there isn't any problem if you eat just a little extra protein. Experts do not recommend eating more than twice the RDA, though. Too much protein in the diet can be dangerous.

The extra protein contains nitrogen, which is changed

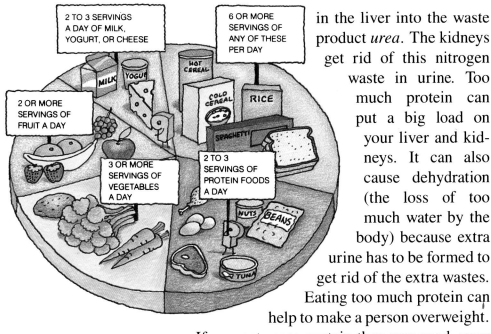

2 TO 3 SERVINGS A DAY OF MILK, YOGURT, OR CHEESE

6 OR MORE SERVINGS OF ANY OF THESE PER DAY

2 OR MORE SERVINGS OF FRUIT A DAY

3 OR MORE SERVINGS OF VEGETABLES A DAY

2 TO 3 SERVINGS OF PROTEIN FOODS A DAY

in the liver into the waste product *urea*. The kidneys get rid of this nitrogen waste in urine. Too much protein can put a big load on your liver and kidneys. It can also cause dehydration (the loss of too much water by the body) because extra urine has to be formed to get rid of the extra wastes. Eating too much protein can help to make a person overweight.

If you eat more protein than you need, your liver will change the excess into fat, which is stored in the body. Being overweight increases your risk of developing health problems such as heart disease and cancer.

Health Problems From Not Consuming Enough Protein

For people in the Third World, the problem often is too little protein, not too much. Each year millions of people die from starvation. Many more fall victim to diseases because they are weakened by poor nutrition. Growing children are especially hard hit. Even if they survive, their physical and mental growth may be stunted.

Some people don't get enough nutrients because they are dieting. Others get enough calories but still suffer from malnutrition because their diet does not provide enough of the right kinds of protein. This can happen when people live on a diet of corn or rice, or when they eat mainly junk foods like donuts, soft drinks, and potato chips.

Do you know what you're eating?

How many grams of protein and how many total calories do these meals supply? (Use the chart of food values on pages 40–41 to figure it out.)

Orange juice, cornflakes with milk and banana, milk.
Bacon and eggs, toast (white bread), milk.
Peanut butter and jelly sandwich, milk.
Tuna salad with celery and salad dressing, lettuce and tomato, milk.
Hamburger on a bun with ketchup and onions, french fries, milkshake.
Steak, baked potato, green beans, lettuce and tomatoes, chocolate ice cream.
Broiled cod, corn, broccoli, roll and butter, applesauce, milk.
Spaghetti with tomato sauce, eggplant, broccoli, peaches, tea.
Turkey with stuffing, cranberries, sweet potatoes, peas, pumpkin pie, milk.

Eating Right

You'll need to do some detective work to make wise food choices. Food package labels give you some important clues. Here is how you figure them out:

Ingredients are listed in order, from the largest amounts to the smallest. (What do you think of the quality of a food that lists "sugar" as one of the first ingredients?) *Nutrients* such as protein, carbohydrates, and fats are given in grams per serving. To figure out the percentage of protein calories, multiply the grams of protein by four, divide the answer by the total calories, and multiply by 100.

For example, a popular brand of snack cracker lists the following nutritional information:

Serving size	*8 crackers (approx. $^1/_2$ oz.)*
Calories	76
Protein	1 g
Carbohydrate	9 g
Fat	4 g

The calorie percentages of each nutrient work out to about 5 percent protein, 47 percent carbohydrate, and 47 percent fat. How do these numbers compare to the nutritional guidelines? Would eating the crackers with butter improve the balance or make it worse? What about a glass of milk?

By being aware of the foods you eat, you can make sure your body gets the nutrients it needs to stay healthy.

Nutritional Values of Common Foods

Food		Portion Size	Protein (g)	Total Calories
Applesauce (sweetened)	1	cup	traces	195
Bacon	3	pieces	6	109
Banana	1	banana	1	105
Broccoli (raw)	1	cup	3	24
Bun (hamburger)	1	bun	3	114
Butter	1	tablespoon	traces	100
Cake (devil's food)	1	piece	3	227
Celery	1/2	cup	traces	10
Cod (baked w/butter)	3 1/2	ounces	23	132
Coffee	1	cup	traces	4
Cookies (choc. chip)	2	cookies	1	99
Corn (cooked on cob)	1	ear	3	83
Cornflakes	1 1/4	cups	2	110
Cranberry sauce (jellied)	1/2	cup	traces	209
Eggplant (boiled)	1/2	cup	traces	13
Eggs (boiled)	1	large	6	79
French fries	10	fries	2	158
Green beans (boiled)	1/2	cup	1	22
Hamburger (broiled)	3 1/2	ounces	24	289
Hot dog (beef)	1	frank (2 ounce)	5	142
Ice cream (chocolate)	1/2	cup	6	280
Jelly	1	tablespoon	traces	49
Ketchup	1	tablespoon	traces	16
Lettuce (iceberg)	1	cup	1	7

Nutritional Values of Common Foods

Food	Portion Size		Protein (g)	Total Calories
Milk (whole)	1	cup	8	150
Milkshake (chocolate)	1	cup	9	230
Onions (raw)	1/2	cup	1	27
Orange juice	1	cup	2	111
Peaches	1	peach	1	37
Peanut butter	1	tablespoon	5	95
Peas (boiled)	1/2	cup	4	67
Potato (baked w/peel)	1	potato	5	220
Pumpkin pie	1	piece	9	367
Roll (dinner)	1	roll	2	85
Salad dressing (mayo.)	1	tablespoon	traces	57
Spaghetti	1	cup	5	155
Steak (sirloin)	3	ounces	23	240
Stuffing (bread)	1	cup	9	416
Sweet potatoes (baked)	1	potato	2	118
Tea	1	cup	0	2
Toast (white bread)	1	slice	2	64
Tomatoes	1	tomato	1	24
Tomato juice	1	cup	2	42
Tomato sauce	1/2	cup	2	37
Tuna (in water)	3	ounces	25	111
Tuna (in oil)	3	ounces	25	169
Turkey (light meat)	3 1/2	ounces	30	157

GLOSSARY

actin—a protein in muscles.

albumin—a protein in blood.

amino acids—the building blocks of proteins. Human proteins contain twenty kinds of amino acids: alanine, arginine, asparagine, aspartic acid, cysteine, glutamic acid, glutamine, glycine, histidine*, isoleucine*, leucine*, lysine*, methionine*, phenylalanine*, proline, serine, threonine*, tryptophan*, tyrosine, and valine*. The nine *essential amino acids* (those our bodies cannot make from other chemicals), are marked with an asterisk.

antibodies—proteins that attack germs that invade the body.

collagen—a protein that helps to hold body cells together.

complements—foods that provide a complete protein when eaten together.

complete proteins—food proteins containing all the essential amino acids.

DNA (deoxyribonucleic acid)—the chemical that holds the instructions for making proteins.

elastin—a stretchy protein found in blood vessels.

enzymes—proteins that help other chemicals to react.

fibrin—protein fibers that help to form a blood clot.

hemoglobin—the colored protein in red blood cells.

hormones—chemical messengers that help to regulate body activities.

hydrochloric acid—a strong acid found in gastric juice (the digestive fluid in the stomach).

incomplete proteins—proteins that do not supply enough of all the essential amino acids.

keratin—a protein in skin, hair, and nails.

mucin—a protein that forms a slippery protective coating in the stomach.

myosin—a protein in muscles.

nutrients—necessary food substances, such as proteins.

peptide—a compound formed when the amino part of one amino acid joins with the acid part of another. Long chains of peptides form a protein.

RDA (recommended dietary allowance)—the amount of a nutrient that experts say a person of a particular age, sex, and weight should eat each day.

rhodopsin—a protein in the eyes that helps in vision.

urea—the nitrogen-containing waste product made from protein in the liver.

U.S. RDA—the recommended daily allowance: the amount of a nutrient needed for good health (a value suitable for most people, based on the RDA).

FOR FURTHER READING

Cobb, Vicki. *More Science Experiments You Can Eat.* New York: Lippincott, 1979.

Cobb, Vicki. *Science Experiments You Can Eat.* New York: Lippincott, 1972.

O'Neill, Catherine. *How and Why: A Kid's Book About the Body.* Mount Vernon, N.Y.: Consumer Reports Books, 1988.

Ontario Science Center. *Foodworks.* Toronto: Kids Can Press, 1986.

Our Body: A Child's First Library of Learning. Alexandria, Va.: Time Life Books, 1988.

INDEX